CAPTURED

by

LONG

ICY

WINTER

Also by Margery McManus Leach
Unexpected Harvest
Sanctuary in Phoenix!
On Being Born Again and Again

CAPTURED BY

LONG ICY

WINTER

POEMS FROM GLOUCESTER, MASS

Margery McManus Leach

Order this book online at www.trafford.com
or email orders@trafford.com

Most Trafford titles are also available at major online book retailers.

© 2010 by Margery McManus Leach. All rights reserved.

Cover image by Dale Partiss Greene
Cover and interior design by Kathleen Valentine
"Long Icy Winter" photograph courtesy of Joyce Mosher
"Tulips" photograph courtesy of John Pries
"Silver Lining" photograph courtesy of Joyce Mosher
All rights reserved. No part of this publication may be reproduced, stored in a retrieval system, or transmitted, in any form or by any means, electronic, mechanical, photocopying, recording, or otherwise, without the written prior permission of the author.

Printed in the United States of America.

ISBN: 978-1-4269-3762-0 (sc)

Our mission is to efficiently provide the world's finest, most comprehensive book publishing service, enabling every author to experience success. To find out how to publish your book, your way, and have it available worldwide, visit us online at www.trafford.com

Trafford rev. 09/08/2010

 www.trafford.com

North America & international
toll-free: 1 888 232 4444 (USA & Canada)
phone: 250 383 6864 ♦ fax: 812 355 4082

For

Donald

who first brought me to Gloucester
sixty years ago
on the Labor Day Weekend
after we married
never hinting
how much treasure I would find.

Preface/Acknowledgements

Writing poetry is another unexpected turn in this faith driven writer's life that has been filled with surprises. After my husband Donald Leach's death, as a retired librarian I became engaged in challenging peace activism. From our family home in Rochester, New York, church sponsored seminars took me to Pacific Islands, Korea, Philippines, and China. Various later humanitarian delegations included Guatemala, Cuba and Chiapas, Mexico. Following eighteen years in Arizona, I thought the excitement would fade away when I moved permanently to Gloucester, Massachusetts, a seaside community of great beauty near my married children.

I am extremely grateful to Ray McGinnis for lighting the spark that eventually resulted in *Captured by Long Icy Winter*. It was after a workshop led by McGinnis, author of *Writing the Sacred – A Psalm-inspired Path* and sponsored by Gloucester's Trinity Congregational Church in the fall of 2007, that my occasional poem writing became a stream of more than words. A second major motivator was the venerable Jim Kelly, my cousin, who from the first poem I included in a Christmas message, insisted that I continue writing poems and send him every one. He even enclosed postage money to prove his sincerity! Another welcome incentive came from John Ronan, poet Laureate of Gloucester, when he interviewed me on the local cable TV program "The Writer's Block."

More thanks go to David Chorlton, editor and Phoenix based poet, who also edited my first autobiography, *Unexpected Harvest*. His keen insight provided a fitting order for the batches of poems I sent him for scrutiny. I am grateful for the publication of several poems in the Trinity Congregational Church bulletin, *The Fisherman,* as well as the *Gloucester Daily Times* "Poets' Corner."

I am especially grateful to Dale Partiss Greene and Kathleen Valentine whose joint artistic efforts (Greene for image and Valentine for cover design) succeeded in pulling together an evocative cover that fit my desires. Additional thanks go to Kathleen Valentine for inside covers and final editing. My appreciation also goes to Kim Howlett-Phillips for back cover and inside author photographs, John Pries for "Tulips" and my daughter, Joyce Mosher, for "Long Icy Winter" and

"Silver Lining" at Stage Fort Park.

Space does not permit naming all the readers who have encouraged me, but a few are cited on the "Readers Comment" page.

ILLUSTRATIONS

Cover image: Dale Partiss Greene

Author photos: Kim Howlett-Phillips

Book One: "Long Icy Winter" courtesy of Joyce Mosher

Book Two: " Garden Tulips" courtesy of John Pries

Book Three: "Half Moon Bench with Silver Lining" courtesy of Joyce Mosher

Contents

Book One – Long Icy Winter   1

1.	Easter	2
2.	My Heartfelt Psalm/Prayer	3
3.	What A Mess!	4
4.	Living Water*	5
5.	Creation	6
6.	Two Views Of My Father	7
7.	Why I Love The Woods	9
8.	Mother Mine	10
9.	Clouds	13
10.	Michigan Jim	14
11.	Beyond Orion	15
12.	New Thoughts On Creation	17
13.	Land	19
14.	Majestic Pine	21
15.	I Went To The Door	22
16.	No Mess Is This	23
17.	Hot Chocolate	24
18.	Promising Spring	25
19.	Oh Happy Birds	26
20.	Praise For Windows	27
21.	The Cardinal Sings	29
22.	I Know It's Spring	31
23.	Rain Bubbles	32
24.	Fog	33
25.	February Thaw For Lincoln's Birthday	35
26.	Pollution	36
27.	Psalm 46:10 – Variations	37
28.	Centering Prayer	38
29.	Bird Count	39
30.	Listening On Thanksgiving Morning	40
31.	Scriptural Prayer	41

32.	For New Widow	43
33.	Autumn Leaves	44
34.	Under Cloudy Sky	45
35.	Sometime Brook	46
36.	Evening Watch By Back Door	47
37.	Fear Not	48
38.	Acrostic Poem Of Praise	51
39.	Saturday Morning	52
40.	Sunday Afternoon Stage Fort Park	53
41.	Cressy's Beach	54
42.	Snowbound Days	55
43.	Tonight	56
44.	Christmas Eve Morning	57
45.	Black Pearls	58
46.	Postscript Can't Wait To Celebrate	60

Book Two – From the Garden of My Life   63

47.	Long Winter Over	64
48.	Thirty-Nine Tulips	65
49.	My Little Cubby	66
50.	Spring Fever	67
51.	Three Goldfinch	68
52.	Easter Season	69
53.	Blessed Assurance	70
54.	Oh For A Birthday In May	73
55.	Light In The Window	75
56.	Welcome Home	76
57.	Joy In The Morning	77
58.	My Bower	78
59.	Lilacs And Wet Woods	80
60.	Silent Moment - News Photo	81
61.	Clang, Clang Went The Pans	82
62.	Tears Of Joy	84
63.	In The Garden—Reunion 2009	85
64.	Token	87
65.	As Summer Retreats	88

66.	Two Sunny Mornings	89
67.	September Morning	90
68.	Long Ago	92
69.	One World	93
70.	Apology	94
71.	Will I Remember?	95
72.	To My Hosts: Angela and Jesse	97
73.	Jesse's Tank	98
74.	Billowing Cloud	99
75.	Oh, Isabel!	101
76.	Perfect Perch	103

Book Three – Silver Linings   105

77.	The Silver Lining	106
78.	This Is The Spot	107
79.	Dear, Dear Friend	108
80.	My Locust Tree	110
81.	Something New	111
82.	Ask Mr. Walton	113
83.	Orion's Return	115
84.	Crows Call	116
85.	Moonlight Sonata	118
86.	November 2009	120
87.	Rubies In Hiding	121
88.	Silver Sheath	122
89.	Early Blessed Assurance	123
90.	I Could Write A Hundred Poems	124
91.	You Must Wait	125
92.	Ravenswood Haven	126
93.	Red Velvet	129
94.	Moonlight With Wilma	131
95.	After The Storm	132
96.	Spring Sunset For Priscilla	133
97.	Half Moon Beach	134
98.	Death Of A Tree	136
99.	Empty Spaces	138

100. Opportunity — 139
101. Postscript : I Must Walk In The Rain — 140
102. Readers Comment — 143

Book One
Long, Icy Winter

PROLOGUE: EASTER

As I prepare this Easter greeting,
slices of my life while still alive,
I wonder, will they be buried
as mementos of grandmother
who lived so long ago
then resurrected when
you are eighty-five?

Will they have any meaning
for you in twenty-five?
What will the world be like?
Will there still be a land of the free?
Will it be destroyed by human disregard?
Or will it survive only in memory?

I can leave nothing more certain
than the joy I feel with God
who made a world
full of beauty and love.
No matter what your trials,
hang on to that.

MY HEARTFELT PSALM/PRAYER

Gracious and loving God over all,
tell me,
How can I serve you now?
Physical and mental powers fade,
but my soul cries out in joy
with each new day.
Yet this is not enough to clutch
for self alone,
the golden leaves that surprised me
at dawn outside my window;
the full-faced moon tonight
rising between trees
just beyond the church.

And now, here, a circle of seekers
'round the room
make for community,
hope for tomorrow,
a legacy for youth.

My mind wanders . . .
in search of what?
I know not.
Lead me on.

WHAT A MESS!

I don't know when my life
became so untidy.
It just sneaked up on me.
Weeks of writing
celestial thoughts
as I wandered through the days
talking to my maker. . .

Papers here and
papers there with
folders on the floor
a little dust between.
The mail arrived.
How to answer, I cannot think
adding more confusion.
My bed is still unmade
and dishes fill the sink.

I await computer helper
whom I cannot comprehend
to kick a virus out
while more and more pile up.
When will this clutter end?

I would not trade
these moments of bliss
for tidiest dwelling ever.
But where, dear God
in all this mess
have we left my glasses?

LIVING WATER*

On my morning walk
a moment comes
when I feel the water of life
filling my cup.
It gives me strength.
It lifts me through the day.

But by evening
my portion is almost gone.
It is time to watch
the sparkling sky,
with its promise for tomorrow
and maybe, even more…

*John 4:10

CREATION

As a child of five or six
I stood at the edge of the road,
my cousin's farmhouse nearby,
a vast cornfield and dense wood
was on the opposite side
covered in heavenly blue.
Only a train whistled by.

I thought of the noisy city
I called home;
houses, flats, apartments
all in a row;
autos, trucks, and streetcars
humming, honking, rattling by.

The haunting sound of trains
linked both our worlds and beyond.
I wondered at those different spheres
and if God, or I, could create others unlike
what I already knew
where we could all share
each other's lives.

I thought and thought on that farm
and when the night train whistle blew
across my city far.
As hard as I tried I could not view
outside what I already new.

From time to time I pondered again
as I grew, but had to accept
that God's mind
was greater than mine.

TWO VIEWS OF MY FATHER

My father was agnostic,
he claimed.
Bible myths he disdained
and advised,
"Don't clutter our mind."

But at six I defied him.
Went to church school,
heard stories of Jesus,
sang hymns and
made friends.

A loving father
of intellectual bent,
he read Darwin and Rousseau
and was non-violent,
no spanking for me.
My conscience instead
would keep me from trouble
he said.

* * *

But later I found
the freedom to live as we please
may bring sorrow, distress and disease.
Drink ruled his life
and his actions, not theories
left our lives in the rubble.

From the soil I arose,
a tender shoot among others,
nourished and grew
seeking cover.

Christ is my haven.
of that I'm aware.
But God's love abides
in all those who care.

MY FATHER
C.E. MCMANUS OR
WHY I LOVE THE WOODS

Into the woods we went.
I was not yet nine.
The winter was cold
and he, without a job,
tried to explain the world to me
in that quiet secluded spot
devoid of people,
leaves or even grass.

A frozen pond
amongst bare trees
has marked the spot
that's carried me
through years of hard times,
resentment, anger, distrust.

And pity, oh, yes, later pity
as his body wasted away,
eyes became sad
and voice was stilled.
Yet his hand scribbled on
with notes of advice,
"Use your head, Girl," his last.
No churchman he.

It was decades after he died
when on a long highway I cried
in wonder and amazement
at what a blessing he'd been
exporting knowledge, tolerance,
love of music, beauty,
the urge to write and the woods.
Oh, the woods.

MOTHER MINE
April 2, 2009

Oh, Mother mine,
Let us sit and have a chat.
It's been almost seventy years
since we have done that.

I see you by the line
hanging clothes blowing in the wind.
The sun is out, the grass is green,
dots of yellow dandelions
grace the scene.

Oh mother mine, I know
your life was full of sadness.
You hardly ever laughed
yet brought me so much
gladness.

On warm summer days
we strolled to the park.
I did somersaults on lawn.
You sat and read beside a bush.
On hotter days with picnic lunch,
we took two streetcars
and a ferry to the riverside.

Belle Isle was paradise;
swings beneath trees,
gaily decorated canoes sliding
under quaint, arched bridges;
at eventide the magic
of a rainbow fountain
and concert under a shell.

In winter cold and wet,
I came inside.
You took my damp clothes
as I shivered over the heat grate
and brought me hot chocolate.
Yummy!

Our trips downtown
on Saturday afternoon
were another delight,
Central Park shaded by trees,
with tall buildings all around.
We moved through aisles of perfume,
yard goods and ribbons,
lunched on hotdogs with buns
with time to listen
as handsome young man
played "Carolina Moon"
on grand piano,
all over too soon.

I see you pumping treadle
making dresses of yellow,
pink and green,
a coat of navy blue,
cut from Grandmother's
older, larger one.

Better than sensual pleasures
and physical care, you fostered
independence and adventure.
I wandered city streets alone,
joined after-school gymnastics
and drama.

When you knew you would not live
much longer, you pleaded strongly

that I not marry before nineteen.
I knew your words were wise,
but my world was so empty without you,
I soon did otherwise.

I've been more obedient
most of the time,
but if I've been good,
it is because
words you said at four,
I took to heart.
"An inner voice
will be your guide
to tell you right from wrong."

You followed Dad's lead
and seldom went to church.
But when I was ten
he left us in the lurch.
In a strange new city
you saw my discomfort,
urged me to go by myself
to the church of my choice.
I've gone ever since.
Wherever I was, you were with me
all along, you and God,
Mother Mine.

CLOUDS
Fall 1977

Clouds fill the sky.
The rain falls.
My heart overflows
and tears roll.

I want to scream
I want to shout
I want to call
my beloved out.

Where has he gone?
Can he see me still?
No, let him be
painless for eternity.

Or let him see
I love him still
no matter what
the pain for me.

How short his life
How filled with good
Let it shine
now in mine.

Oh, Donald of the soft brown eyes
gentle voice, and loving care
that made this earthly life
for me almost paradise.

How can I clutch what we just had,
hold it closely, nurture it,
then let it go to bloom again
in some unknown way,
beyond my ken?

MICHIGAN JIM
April 2009

Michigan Jim has traveled far and wide
mostly with Janet at his side.
It's different now, more difficult,
but fond memories still abide.
With a slower pace,
other places have been tried.

Woods still comfort and sustain
through sunshine, wind and rain.
His sons matured, grandchildren too.
Laws and torts were left behind,
but unsolved problems still remain
of politics and miscellaneous pain,
needing less muscle, more brain.

The outward-inward dance goes on:
people follies, society pitfalls,
What is right and what is wrong?
Which is weakness? Which is strength?
Why can't we just all get along?

Modest sage of Smith Creek,
comfort of widows,
I salute you, cousin, keep buzzin'!

No April Fool,
Happy Birthday!
Gerry

BEYOND ORION

Four windows bring light
into my back room slumber space.
Two look south, the others west.

During milder seasons
foliage of great trees block
the night time sights both ways.
But oh, the glories of the cold
when Orion flies the skies
across my southern view.

Back to Conneaut I am born
now stargazing with Dad,
home at Grandmother's house,
from a long job hunting trek
across the nation wide.

What a wondrous treat
to walk the sandy shore at eventide,
to gaze above at the changing dome,
yet recite so yearningly:

"Twinkle, twinkle little star.
How I wonder what you are
up above the world so high. . ."
ending nightly with fervent wish,
Please dear God,
find my daddy a job!

Seventy plus years have passed.
Other children come to mind.
Have their parents lost jobs?
Have they lost their homes?
Has someone taken them in?

Or are they cold and hungry,
looking longingly
on high?

As hard as such times are,
new delights come to treasure,
like searching sky in clear weather.
Please dear God,
grant each as much as I.

NEW THOUGHTS ON CREATION

Ah, yes, God's mind
was greater than mine.
But how did I fit in all this?

With help from my maker
through many blessings,
much turmoil and death,
husbands and children,
I tried to manage
without damaging
the shoots from our roots.
In my distress I sought knowledge
tending books in college and career
until husbands and children had flown,
my mates to heaven and offspring
to lives of their own.

Once again I was restless.
God responded with a quest
that reminded of search in the past
for a different world.

Though God was wiser,
the different world I sought
and thought sealed,
needed to be revealed.
Every ingredient was already here.
But those who inhabited
God's magnanimous gift
required a nudge, yes, from me
to help them see
how we may endure adversity,
caring for one other.

Would you believe?
I was led far away
from my sheltered home
and congenial job
East of China and Korea,
to bring back word
of good and generous people
still suffering in the far Pacific
from burning ash
of U.S. testing blast!

LAND
February 9, 2003

This land
your land
my land
Native American land
preserve it;
conserve it;
it deserves it.

In fear, bombs, missiles
is no security.
Schools deprived
guns survive.
impure water
unclean air,
let's show some maturity.

Endless war
seeking terrorists
can never please,
a solution worse
than the disease.

We can't control it.
We can't afford it.
A world aflame
we cannot tame.

US cannot survive
lest it contrive
to share our bounty
with others.
Stop robbing brothers.

That land
of the Bantu,
Koreans, Hindustani,
preserve it.
Their children deserve it.

That land of the Iraqis,
preserve it.
Their children deserve it.

NO WAR PLEASE!

MAJESTIC PINE

What can you tell me, Majestic Pine?
With lower limbs chopped
for a telephone line,
your feathered fronds above
stretched beneath the pale half moon,
waving gently, whisper softly,
"Yes, we're still here.
Tarry a bit while we soothe
restless, cooped up feelings.
There's time for those
when you've feasted
on our splendrous ware."

Across the path, a glacial erratic stands
twice my height and reach.
Sparkling from our ancient sun
its granite snow-capped helm
sends thoughts beyond
to your unending realm.

I WENT TO THE DOOR

I went to the door
to start each day
in gratitude and wonder.
Looking up at the scene before me,
a snow laden hillside is sketched
in granite and dark bark.

All is silent.
Even the birds
are beyond sight and sound.
Just you and me, God, all around.
Rapturously I stand.

Then glancing down,
I see faint shovel tracks.
My young neighbor has prepared
a way for me.

So too at the front of the house,
I soon discover
another has cleared
from the driveway to front door.
I have a choice!

But which way to go?
Showered with riches,
it is so hard to decide.
Lead me. Lord.

NO MESS IS THIS

Lured outside to see my yard
of shrinking snow, spreading green,
I see more rocks cutting
through the glacial landscape.
Lumpy ground, crumbling wall,
spruce barren half way up,
not a tidy scene.
But where oh where is
my sometime brook?

Disgusted to spot
what I think to be trash
I hazard a few steps
on slippery ground and find
no waste, but sculptured ice
made by fallen twigs
across the path,
tiny droplets molded
into exquisite
marble drapery!

What wondrous things
nature has wrought!
Surely too, inside clutter
of my house
can be seen as part
of work of art
not quite done.

HOT CHOCOLATE

It's almost March.
I've muddled through
this icy, snow laden winter.
More will come on Tuesday,
but the walk is clear
around the ellipse of a parking lot
across from Stage Fort Park.

Wind bites my cheeks
and rumbles under the brim of my hat
as it meets me
coming over the hill
off the sea by Cressy's beach.
I love that kind of god
that after hours inside
brings fresh, fresh air.

Seagulls, crows and other life
live here all the time.
But creatures of the mind
hibernate in heated dwellings
express concern about
lack of care for God's
magnificent house.

When I return
a great wind begins to roar.
Trees rock and pine needles whir.
I am glad not to be along the shore
but drinking hot chocolate
at home.

PROMISING SPRING

Oh, thank you God
for my Sometime Brook
once again bubbling
down a woodland trench
singing its story,
assuring the world is alive
promising the freshness of spring.

For the first time since fall
I eat my lunch
on the sunny porch table.
I feast too on
lacy patches of snow
that garnish with relish
emerging land below.

OH HAPPY BIRDS

Oh happy birds,
the storm is over.
The sun shines brightly
beneath bare lilac branches
where jays and sparrows
munch and mingle
upon the snow

But I must shovel the porch roof
or melting drift will leak
forcing repairs
when I want only shade!

PRAISE FOR WINDOWS

Praise the windows of this house
with a view of the curve below,
motor traffic rounding the bend
as joggers brave the wind.
Lights from Strong's garage
assure plows are busy
on stormy nights.

Praise the upstairs window
looking east where in winter
I watch the sky change
as sun sneaks across the graveyard hill.
Praise back west windows
when moonlight shines
between bare tree trunks
casting shadows
on snowy slopes.

Praise porch windows
that lead my eyes
up the path into the wood.
Praise, too, the window
where from the computer I spy
callers at back door.

Praise bath window
when snow high on the ground
brings busy birds
crunching seed
my neighbor supplies.
Praise that small opening again
in spring when the scent and sight
of lilacs enchant me
through the hours.

Praise God for home
that provides
shelter and delight
whatever the season,
windows into the soul.

THE CARDINAL SINGS

The sun is warm on my back.
The grass is soft under foot.
"Pretty, pretty, pretty chirps
the cardinal I cannot spot
though trees are still bare.

I tread the ivy path into the wood
to find my sometime brook,
now just a trickle amongst dead leaves.
The big gnarled oak still stands,
and the red bird sings on.

Not until I return to steps and
stretch my neck directly above,
does his tiny scarlet form
pierce blue sky and say,
Yes, spring is on the way!

Step by step the long icy winter
stalked across the land
halting traffic and timid feet,
closing schools, stopping planes.
Still, life goes on.

Even long icy winters
have their blessings!
Cozy meetings at the pastor's house,
a dozen or so seeking souls
gather weekly to ponder
"Spiritual Direction,"
Henri Nouwen's words,
"Wisdom for the Long Walk of Faith."

We read, we pray,
we share our thoughts.
Intimately we talk of
God in our lives.

And through the winter long
I'm grabbed by muse of the poet
seeing signs of God everywhere.

I KNOW IT'S SPRING

I know it's spring because
the peachy glow at daybreak
has moved from graveyard
east behind houses on the hill.
Tulip bulbs planted by my son
by granite wall and trellis are
peeking through rusty leaves.

Yes, the long, icy winter
has limited activity.
Yet hours have been filled
in close community
where we've shared
our spiritual hunger
and alone in joyous creativity.

Orion may leave our view
and leaves blot out the rest,
but warm weather
will bring us waterside
where skies are open wide.
The Cut will have its spectators
with cars waiting to cross
as boats sail in and out of the sea.

The world goes round,
but we are not upside down.
We cannot have it all,
but with an attitude of gratitude
all we have can be the best.

RAIN BUBBLES

Clutching a high bathroom sill
watching birds on lingering snow
my attention was diverted
to bubbles on the roof below.

My mind went back
to a summer long ago
when I first marveled
at the gutter sprouting bubbles
as I watched the heavens burst.

How I longed to run outside
and catch them! But Mama said "No."
Pleasure may be fleeting,
just moments passing by.
Still, if you notice,
its charm goes on forevermore.

FOG

Evening fog in late March
lights up the city sky
beyond the Annisquam.
Mournful tone of horn
holds no fear for me.
Its low music speaks
of days gone by
when Donald was here
and in his quiet way
showed me wonders
that are Gloucester,
Cape Ann, and so much more.

We vacationed with our children,
his parents and all their kin,
taking in the beaches,
going for a swim.
We prowled the docks
around the harbor
watched the catch come in.
Empty masts stand stately
home at last
lined up along the bay.

Here I am back again,
alone alas,
soaking up the marvels
of this community, its past.
Our children live nearby,
grandchildren and greats too,
except for one who joins us
now and then.
We live our different lives,
but will come together soon.

Growing in awareness
of others here and there,
we strive our best
to dwell in harmony.
God give us strength,
will and love
to bind us to each other,
and all humanity.

HAPPY MEMORIAL DAY

FEBRUARY THAW FOR LINCOLN'S BIRTHDAY
February 12, 2009

Rock remnants of an ice age
expose their shapes
as a snow carpet recedes
down the steep back slope.
Once more my tiny brook
rushes gaily from barren spot
to sluice below.

No, it is not spring.
Ice still lurks
beneath sun softened snow.
And more will fall
until once again heavenly white
buries all.

This fairyland of forest
is my winter prize
shared with chickadees and squirrels,
bright cardinals and jays.
But traffic noise reminds
that breakfast calls.

POLLUTION
1960s

Years have past since I stood
gazing at a barren attic wood,
imagining the patter of little feet,
the sound of voices young and sweet.
I saw walls and beds, toys and games,
schoolbooks scribbled
with children's names.

Today, I swam in the sunlit pool
in water not quite so clean
as when we first built it
and laughter filled it.
Life was serene.

All this in time must cease;
but must this be a haunted house
where silent footsteps duck in and out?
Joy and mirth once filled the air;
now rejection, doubt, despair.
Must this be a house of gloom
where caution and suspicion
cloud every room?
Have disdain, hedonism, or fear
conquered love, warmth, hope, and cheer?

2009

Years more have past
since that day of frustration.
Read on and enjoy my elation!

PSALM 46:10 – VARIATIONS

Be still and know that I am God.
I have made you
from the tips of your toes
to the thoughts in your head.

I have called you by name,
out of the dark winter of the womb
into a world of words.

Be still and know that I am.
I have called you by name
and you have answered me.

I won't be ashamed of you
no matter what you do.
I will love you forever.
This isn't a game,
but a circle of seekers
each calling my name.

CENTERING PRAYER

At home alone we take time for
contemplative prayer.
Then I leave the table
to exercise on the floor,
which is carefully covered with
Philippine cloth.

I have carried it the world over,
with brightly colored symbols of life,
birds, leaves and flowers
of gold and tangerine
on bed of almond seeds
over mossy green.

As I go down to the floor that day,
I'm astounded by a thought -
this is the way Muslims pray.
I lower my head all the way,
touching the fabric reverently.
Tears of joy engulf me
as in the most moving
moments of my life.
Kneeling at prayer
I don't usually do
and am carried back
to Philippine Islands and
all that followed.

I wait, absorbed in the moment
observing myself bent over
cherished souvenir
where I will lie stretching
each limb to keep going,
doing whatever needs to be done.
The soft music turns more joyful.
I will dance before I lie down again.

BIRD COUNT

What have I seen
this stormy day before noon?
A song sparrow with not a tune,
cardinals, blue jays and
mourning doves,
starlings, pigeons and a titmouse,
chickadees, nuthatch, and a
pair of downy woodpeckers
enlivened my watch.

Ooh, rarest of all,
a red-bellied woodpecker
with no red on his belly, but
lots on neck and head..
Where did he come from
and why no squirrels?
Did they see the crowd
and go back to bed?

LISTENING ON THANKSGIVING MORNING
November 23, 2008

Into the woods
expectant I went
beholding barren trees,
mossy rocks, and pebbled paths
all silent and still.

"Listen!" my instructions were
"Praise God" I heard the tall ones say.
"We furnish shelter and shade,
a chapel to nourish your spirit."

"Listen! Then go out into the world
among the people
and listen again."

Knowing my reluctance to leave
the rock seat where I wrote,
a crow called "Go!"
and I went.

***

What a feast of family and food followed!
But silently I sat
until asked to offer Grace.
What could I say? I paused and
after joyous thanks for the gathering, I recalled:
"Into the woods, expectant I went . . ."

SCRIPTURAL PRAYER

Your will be done.
Matthew 6:10
Be still and know that I am God.
Psalm 46:10a
*and have your lamps lit . . .
take time to be ready*
Luke 12:32-40

Time to be ready turned into
time to share
with our hospitalized members
and then a neighbor friend.
This included a poem about
the centering prayer group.

After a bit she asked,
"Tell me Marge, why are we
talking about God and prayer?"
This shook me a bit
until I realized I had trodden
on her private God space.
I had to come to grips with rejection,
then remembered my hospital friends
who craved for more.

Next day after centering time,
I delayed breakfast
to absorb what was happening.
I needed to go outside
to feel the cold, crisp air.
I watched swaying trees still bare,
And listened to crows
high in the sky.

I fear another friendship is slowly drifting.
Does my concentrated writing
rob her of needed help?
Do I play Mary to her Martha?
With lessening body energy
does her spirit cry out
"I want to be Mary too?"

I go back to scripture:
Your will be done.
Be still and know that I am God.
Have your lamps lit and
- take time to be ready! -

FOR NEW WIDOW

When sorrow and grief
come to the door
sadness and anguish soon follow.

You may greet them with
reluctance, dread and despair,
but patience and faith bring
not only will to survive,
but to live in surprising ways,
God's presence with you
all of your days.

AUTUMN LEAVES

From the back step I watch
autumn leaves hang on.
Some crisp, brilliant in color,
others shriveled, moth-eaten.
Each gives all they can,
one last breath of oxygen.
Slowly falling, they live on
to nourish the earth below
as they did above.

So too does our flesh serve
above and below,
but where or how high
my spirit will soar,
I don't know.

At this late time of life
I feel fertile again.
My body fades,
but my spirit grows.
I think I will burst!

UNDER CLOUDY SKY
November 2008

At rock by first swamp I must stop
to breathe the beauty coming out of dark:
Rusty speckled leaves still hang on
lighting the forest like a Christmas tree.
Broad green strokes on black trunks,
medallions spread from lichen,
and silver water reflecting leaden sky.

My soul is still until I recall
ecstatic joy of the week
when "Free at Last" is proclaimed
by dark lips unloosed from bitter pain;
my childhood memories of
our nation's stain.
I feel it all; the hurt released
and hope fulfilled.
Once again I hear
"You are mine, all belong."
We are one!

As I leave, coming back to earth,
a tribe of blue jays raucous sounds
pierce the silence again.
Then comes a long sweet trill
and across the harbor
a fog horn moans.

SOMETIME BROOK

I watch through a second story window
as tumbling foam
from the early December storm
rushes through a wooded trench.
Down a culvert north bound it goes
past Anderson's stone garage
huddled into the hillside
covered with amber leaves.

It may be spring
before I see this sight again.
What surprises will winter bring?

EVENING WATCH BY BACK DOOR

When the traffic stops
I hear only the trickling brook
making its way above ground.
Sometimes below the surface
it sinks, then rises again
where it mingles with other streams
until at last
it merges with the sea.

My life does that,
gathering with other souls
from different places.
We meet and part
and meet again
until I feel a part of all
creation.

FEAR NOT
October 31, 2009

I couldn't have known
when I started this poem
what a wonderful day
it would end.

At daybreak I had a stiff back
and cramp in one leg
as I dragged my body
out of bed.

I was cheered with thoughts
of calling Diane at nine
to explore Ravenswood once again.
She would prefer afternoon.
Can I solve chapter twenty-eight
while I wait?

Trash and recyclables out,
exercise and breakfast done,
I tackle the trouble spots of
"Father, Faith, Politics and Peace,"
then turn to the mail.

At the doorstep she waits
and off we go
trudging up the hill,
in crisp autumn air.

We trade pieces of our past
then halt, enthralled
by shining leaves.
It is a magical time.
Two lives entwine.

We had bird-watching husbands
now search for new life.
Mine well marked,
hers still in a haze.

Will she read chapter twenty-eight?
In affirmative her reply,
she edited for a major firm.
Back home we part,
manuscript in her hand.

* * *

The doorbell awakens me
to trick-or-treaters,
bags outstretched.
I'm spurred to leave
before more distractions.
I find the church closed,
a night off you see.
No meal this Halloween.

Eating at Thai Choice,
I scribble a beginning;
write more at Gloucester Stage,
"Frozen River," to come.
That film is not to be,
but we are offered,
"Revolution by Music."

I am enraptured by Estonians
as far as eye can see,
fearlessly singing praises
for homeland; for freedom
from Soviet tyranny
relentlessly moving in rhythm
like waves of the sea.

After years of choral evocation,
ominous tanks threaten a tower
but withdraw
as dawn is breaking.

Such a glorious ending
I wish for all oppressed.
No gun fire, no bombs, no torture.
Just humanity singing
to stop the dark from coming.

An ominous election is upon us,
may fear not prompt our choice.

ACROSTIC POEM OF PRAISE

Allow me, oh God, to address you freely.
Because you have heard me and
Called me by name,
Daily I praise you
Each time I am blessed.
Forever will I praise you, O
God.

How can I not?
In the morning your sunlight
Joyously brightens my room.
Keenly,
Lovingly,
My soul greets you in rapture.
No slouch on a couch
Or grouch
Pours out to
Quench the gift of a new day.

Rather than drift back into slumber, I
Stretch my legs
Twenty times or more
Until I can arise
Very stable to reach the
Window and greet you with
e**X**ultation and prayers for peace in
Your world from A to
Zee.

SATURDAY MORNING

Sunshine outside the window
drew me to back door
where glories of winter
flooded my soul-
young blue jays, jet black crows,
tiny titmice and a junco.

Squirrels were having a party.
White snow framed every move,
hopping across the yard
skipping along Elizabeth's railing
jumping through the trees.

SUNDAY AFTERNOON
STAGE FORT PARK

All that glitters is not gold.
Sometimes it's leaves left on trees
when sun is shining
and sky is blue.
That is precious gold
especially for the old.

CRESSY'S BEACH

O the beauty of the eve,
crystal waters,
mound of earth jutting out to sea
as the sinking sun hues the bay
and half moon lights the shore.

As I marvel at such wonders
God speaks to me.
"Be patient, dear."

SNOWBOUND DAYS

Oh Great God,
I should be on my knees
honoring your deeds.
Am I lazy or don't I dare?
My joints, no longer quick, stick
And chores remain undone.

But give me snowbound days
when my mind can wander
and relish in wonder
of how years have sped
leaving such dread.
Now with providence,
I'm overwhelmed by love and beauty,
not duty.

May your grace that's gifted
be sifted, wider
and wider.

TONIGHT

Tonight,
listening to carols
gay and full of yearning,
loved ones of yesterday
pierce my heart.

A sometime stream
rolls down my cheek
tinged with both joy
and sorrow.

Ah, yes,
'tis that time of year
when in the darkest sky
shines the brightest star
to light tomorrow.

Be not sad my soul.
Life is full
no matter where you are.

CHRISTMAS EVE MORNING

Once again it's almost Christmas.
The leaden sky forebodes
beyond the barren trees
in snow upon the hillside
where rocky forms protrude.

Yet was ever this day of promise
more expectantly approached?
My body not as nimble
yet head and spirit thrill
as a troubled world awakens
and democracy unfurls.

Racial barrier shattered
"Si ce puede" we cry!
Together we will do it;
God help us as we try.

HAPPY NEW YEAR 2009!

BLACK PEARLS

The heavy snow lies
in piles along the way.
Without replenishment,
curbside bank is dirty gray.

Yet sunlight turns frozen droplets
to black pearls,
ground with diamonds
pierced with strands of twigs
bronze against the snow.

Once more it is quiet as eternity.
As I search for signs of life,
pine needles flutter high above.

The murmur of homeward traffic
warns that I must hasten
before the day is through
and darkening sky
replaces azure blue.
I have much to do.

"And when you turn to the right
or when you turn to the left,
your ears shall hear a word behind you
saying, "This is the way; walk in it."
Isaiah: 30:21

POSTSCRIPT
CAN'T WAIT TO CELEBRATE
April 23, 2009

There is sound of water flowing
where I am going,
but mostly I hear tap, tapping
of rain drops on dry leaves
and my hat.

It is a charming place
with bushes along the way
covered with green lace.
I wonder what I shall find
on this winding trail,
the first time through since winter.
If it doesn't pour,
I'll make it to the lake shore.

I must not stumble or get lost,
but no longer worry about frost.
I could not wait to celebrate
the rapture that came after
Long, Icy Winter.

On the way back I was startled
by bushy white rear of a deer
which crashed through the woods
and then disappeared.

I stopped to inquire
if deer had such flashy tails.
The good doctor who lived nearby
could give no details on the subject,
instead showed me wonders
he'd wrought after sewer construction
revealed magnificent boulders

dropped eons ago where glacier ended
at the edge of his yard.

I'm welcome to come and explore,
he invited.
Now I'm so excited,
maybe that's where I'll go
the next time I open my door.

Book Two
From the Garden of My Life

Courtesy of John Pries

LONG WINTER OVER

The long icy winter is over
but my muse has not deserted.
Crowded with ideas for dispersal
and hampered by computer,
I am roused from my sloth
and away I go
without the snow.
For five hours straight
I am tugged by fate
while "Blessed Assurance in May"
takes shape.

Now let me rest my eyes again.
In peace and love recline
after I have dined
on granola, calcium and nuts,
fortified by berries and vitamins.
Exercise will have to wait
until I'm in a rested state.

THIRTY-NINE TULIPS

Thirty-nine tulips
and a daffodil,
red, yellow, pink and white
along the gray stone wall.
Wrapped in green
captured by neighbor,
a Spring to remember.

Thank you, Jean!

Margery L.

MY LITTLE CUBBY

My little cubby
with a peak at the sky
above the tree line.

I fondly think of this
when warmer weather
comes and would allow me
to sit on the porch
with forest world
at my feet
and birds that sing,
a favorite treat.

But will I still prefer
this cozy winter spot
to contemplate in prayer,
silently with no distractions
anywhere?

How blessed I am
to have choices
but not to shut out voices
when I seek guidance.

Many thanks again.

SPRING FEVER

A crowd of Blue Jays
greeted me this morning
beneath the bathroom sill.
Never mind that others
say they are a nuisance,
nasty birds.

The shining purple Grackle
and Starling too are there.
But the vibrant blue of Jay
reflects the sky
with white wing strips
on their way
like clouds to spark a fair day.

It's still chilly,
but I pull on
my garden pants
and hat to pull out withered
leaves around the tulips
by the back wall.
Tiny shoots are
coming through to
delight me in May.

THREE GOLDFINCH

Three goldfinches are
outside my window.
Two on feeder
another waits on bough.
Now there are four,
a lone lady finch
waiting to dart
when she can.
'Twas ever thus.

What a sight
to brighten the day
before it is night.
It is hard to tear away
to write.

EASTER SEASON

A babe was born
in a stable long ago
to save us all.
About his life
words have been spread.

He died on barren wood.
He lives on
for all who believe,
drink from his cup,
and eat of his bread.

Some are skeptics,
others haven't heard.
But the dream lives on
in Gandhi,
Martin Luther K. and more.
Say not
such lives are misguided.

I feel born again
with strength to carry on
each time I taste
the love that was given
that I might not waste
God's gifts.

This love is present
for all those who serve
their brothers and sisters
no matter how small the deed
if given in love,
not what we think
they deserve.

BLESSED ASSURANCE

I look at photos
of those in my room
who have brought me a life
now in tune
and glance out the window
as wet springtime unfolds.
I find blessed assurance
and know
as we follow God's way
peace and justice
will also follow
in all the world one day.

I must consecrate this hour.
One more poem
that will be known
for other's grace
from this place.

Blessed Assurance
Jesus is mine,
Oh, what a foretaste
this glory divine.
Blessed assurance
Jesus is ours,
those who walk with us
to follow God's word.
The glory of springtime
each leaf and bud
shower around us
signs of God's love.

Some days have passed
since I was buried in troubles.

Computer crashes
had done me in.
Exhausted and harried
I sank in my chair
quietly waited
with no where to turn.

Out of the silence
jangled the phone-
A new step was offered
as caller replied:
"This is Dell checking;
can I help you today?"
I could have cried.

More choices were offered
I was quick to respond.
In time climbed out
from slough of despond.

This morning I'm joyously
ready to tackle the machine,
but by the back door
I smell moist woods
and return for thick shoes
and a cane.
I sit on new perch
a rock by the stream
feel God's presence
fresh from the rain.

How exquisite the morning-
rocks glistening,
water rippling
new leaves on the trees.
Once again my cup is filled.
It is time to get up,

but wait, how can I share
these moments of bliss?
Who else might I touch
with such blessedness?

I thought of some names-
You've got to do it, I'm told.
That's all there is too it!
And yours is one of them.
May God's peace be with you
in May and evermore.

OH FOR A BIRTHDAY IN MAY

You have heard many times
your name is Joyce
because having a girl
was something to rejoice,
but I wonder
did it take this long
for me to realize
what a grand month is May
in which to be born?

White lilacs outside my window
purple trailing behind
tulips by the back wall.
Now two new rose bushes
at the bottom of the trellis.
The lawn is rich green
and trees spread
their fluttering leaves.
New plantings by your brother
who just happened by
when I was running out of food
too ill to buy more at the store.

Oh, let us stay in May
the whole year through.
But no, should time stand still,
I would not see my lovely daughter
grow and blossom to maturity.

I'm getting soupy now
thinking of what the years have meant
and what more is in store.
I've watched the tables turn
as we have journeyed

from caring for you to
you caring for me.
Thank you.
It's time to stop and wish you

A VERY HAPPY BIRTHDAY IN MAY!

All my love, always,
Mom

LIGHT IN THE WINDOW

I should have been asleep
but the light in the window
across the way
brought my neighbor
to mind.

I'm struggling with a fever
from an unknown source;
she with ominous surgery
on Thursday,
a verdict to bear.

What can I do?
Her burdens are heavy;
mine are light.
God, bless her now
and keep her in Your care.

WELCOME HOME

I woke up this morning
to the most glorious blue sky
with green trees waving below
and sun shining through
the window beside me.

It is cold.
But I am tucked in a warm flannel sheet
covered with my mother-in-law's down quilt
and on the table to greet me
is a friend's peachy begonia.

I am shaky, but oh, so happy!
Thank you God for this morning
and being home again
from a long journey.

I will miss you all this evening,
gathered around the table
at the pastor's house
sharing a meal for our last
Tuesday spirituality meeting.

Still I know the spirit kindled
as we opened our lives
and pondered the Word
will continue burning
not just among us, but
those we touch along the way.

God bless you all.

Margery

JOY IN THE MORNING

The joy I feel
as my wounds heal
from nasty ticks
and fall on the floor
is hard to contain
or explain.

I awaken early
ready to take
up my life again.
Photos on the wall
bring moments to treasure.

There are more to assemble
in coming hours,
words of gratitude to measure
in response to waving leaves
from my bower.

MY BOWER

What is there about this bower
where I sleep and waken
that grabs me so?
Then I remember long ago
a third floor bedroom
where I napped on summer days
watching high trees
wave their leaves at me
as I day-dreamed about
our baby that was to come.

How many more would there be?
Where would Curly and I be living
in later years with our growing brood?
I could imagine a large green lawn
set on a hill with frisky
dogs tumbling with our children.

Those were sweet exciting dreams,
but they were not meant to be.
There were two not one
waiting to be born.
They came too soon,
as did another later one.
Curly, too, passed from my scene
after six long months
of hospital care.

Yes, this bower
has a special poignancy for me,
but so much happiness
has followed along
with the tears and years that passed.
Another loving husband, then

David, Joyce and Douglas
with grandchildren and
great grandchildren too.
I cannot help but see
my new leafy bower as a special
incubator of dreams and heaven.
Thank you God.

LILACS AND WET WOODS

How exquisite the scent
of lilacs and wet woods
as I open the back door
this misty morning.
I can't breathe in enough of it
and would not close the door
but it is so chilly.

Still, I am left remembering
times with Donald
wandering in wet woods.
A trailer park above a lake,
kids all off to camp,
thinking of our future
when we would be alone.

But right then
it was the beauty of the place,
two lives entwined
on a single path
beneath dripping boughs,
God's abundance showers down.

Silent Moment - News Photo
May 29, 2009

So alone
so bare,
corpse in coffin,
faithful sister
bent over long,
tufted satin sofa.

White walls,
bare shiny hardwood floors illuminated by ceiling
chandelier and pair of torch lamps
set in arched and draped alcove
guarding casket.

Another lamp unlit
waiting mourners
to sign the book.

Stark the scene
so tender the love
between ancient sisters,
ninety-two and one hundred
and four years.

Washington Post Weekly Edition
May 18-24, 2009 "Cut Rate Angels"by
Paula Span; Photos by Carol Guzy, p.11

CLANG, CLANG WENT THE PANS

The clang, clang of pans
as I pull them from rack
hanging beneath the sink
would drive some cooks crazy.
Such a clatter!

But I am carried back
above Lake Luzerne
to a Swiss mountain trail and Donald.
We listened to the sweet tinkle
of bells on brown cows
as they lunched among
wild flowers on the countryside.

Our first trip to Europe,
nine countries in twenty-one days,
full of faulty brakes
and numerous delays
nevertheless bring untold
daily delights as my
pans unfold.

Our bus load took a tram
high up the mountainside
while we rode a ferry upon the lake,
stopping off half way down
at a village by the water.
We tramped around up and down
listening to the tinkling bells
then savored hot chocolate in
a quaint café.

A precious time for two alone,
a romantic adventure
away from the crowd.
So too we trod the crooked
streets of Sorrento while
the rest took in Capri.

And later by moonlight
wandered the maze of Venice
listening to gondolier
as companions glided by.

In Greece we wound our way
to the Acropolis and stood
where Saint Paul preached.
Some may have thought us unfriendly,
but our slow pace
was right for us.

TEARS OF JOY

Shall I mourn forever
those lost so long ago?
No, life is too precious,
too full to be ignored

I've shed my tears,
in days long past.
They've watered the
garden of my life,
bringing forth a
field of flowers
as far as eye can see.
When one fades,
another blooms
more vibrant than before.

How can I cry
when God has blessed me so?
'Tis joy, joy, joy
that rules today.
Joy to breathe the moist morning air
Joy to meet the stranger, friend or kin
Joy to seek, to plow for knowledge,
meaning, and Divine
Joy to serve, my heart full beaming.

God grant me one more day.
But if not,
I go with spirit o'er flowing.

IN THE GARDEN—REUNION 2009

I stand here waiting
for Wilma, Herb and Dee,
soaking in the loveliness
of my cousin's garden.

A riot of colors
in rows along the house,
in halos around the trees
visited by blue jays,
cardinals and squirrels
while on velvet green
an orange tabby
watches lazily.

We will walk to Peppers
for our breakfast,
then enjoy the beach.
But I have no urge
to leave this space.
It reminds me of the
glistening colors
in my grandparents' yard,
after a summer storm,
and we as curious children,
later adventurous adults
making contact through the years.

Now we are all over eighty,
still companions along the way,
choosing our adventures
more carefully as agility fades,
but still entranced
with floral and other beauty
as we try to dance
through the days.

Troubles have been plenty,
joyous times too,
clouds along with blue.
While good times seem best,
we learn to love more deeply
from the rest.

TOKEN

A single yellow rose
brightened my morning walk!
The first to bloom since freeze
of five winters past,
gift of a friend.

The label said apricot
of which I am very fond,
but yellow was my mother's favorite.
This scented pale beauty
matches the house
and accents the green trellis
it will climb some time.
Thoughts of the new floral bloom
revived me from usual
after-breakfast slump.
Back to the computer
I jumped!

AS SUMMER RETREATS

A beautiful time of year
is descending upon us.
Pray give me strength
to make the most of it.

Humid heat has given way
to bright skies and mild temperatures,
laundry flapping in the wind
hopefully shooing mosquitoes away.
Ah yes, there are still mosquitoes
and ticks to dampen our pleasure.

But say no more –
eat your breakfast
take a shower
and resume copying poems
of *Long Icy Winter*
for others to enjoy.

Sometime after lunch
head for Beverly
hoping for visit with Isabel,
pray over her bodily trials
and savor our grateful spirits.

TWO SUNNY MORNINGS

I end my breakfast
with more moments of tears.
I know they come so readily now
because my body is not well.
But my spirit, joined with
Dom Camara's words[1*]
make me whole
enough to do my work
praising God's everlasting presence
that shares our sorrows and
helps us sing and dance
through the day.

I began breakfast
taking in the morning's beauty
remembering a similar time
almost forty years ago.
Sitting in a rose garden
anticipating graduation, I was
thrilled to have finally finished
years of formal education,
wondering what the future might bring.

Ah, the future –
it is in each moment
we live and observe
the gifts of the Eternal's presence
even when desperately difficult.

1* "When I give food to the poor I am called a saint.
When I ask why they are poor, I am called a communist."
Dom Elder Camara – *Essential Writings*
[Francis McDonagh]

SEPTEMBER MORNING

The aroma of warm cereal
mixed with fresh morning air
transports me again
to the state of rapture
when I was earlier
hanging clothes on the line.

I'm like a yo-yo, but
more up than down.
Doused with repellant
to scare away bugs
I take childlike delight
in feeling free as the air.

Once again I am with my mother,
glad to be outside
as long as I remain
within her sight.

Oh God, I am with you
wherever I may be
feeling your closeness best
when I am at rest.
Your presence emerges,
gathering me in your arms
squeezing me tight.

My daughter Joyce will bring Eli
and Miss Mollie later today.
I have no idea what we will do
to keep them busy
and out of mosquitoes' way.

Working on poetry
would be easier,
but how can I resist
this rare chance to watch
these jeweled pieces of a future
I may never see?
We observed as Eli tirelessly
built and rebuilt cardboard blocks
while Mollie napped.
Once awake we strolled to the bridge
stuck with cars waiting to pass
and boats stalled on the sea.
A perfect day for time to stand still.
Now, fireworks burst
signaling summer's end.

LONG AGO

Someone must have lived here long ago.
There is a hollow beside the road
filled with low growth.
But around the edges
honeysuckle and lilacs
perfume the air.

A towhee laments their passing
with his "drink your tea-e-e-e."
Great trees behind stifled by vines
hanging like Spanish moss
give a sense of time.

Now I walk this hallowed place
left for wanderers to embrace
by thoughtful citizen of yore.
Thank-you, Mr. Sawyer,
who left a library, too,
food for the mind and
more for the soul.

ONE WORLD

It started with one small sign.
Written on a piece of scrap paper
with ball point pen it proclaimed,
"Fighting Terrorism Since 1492."

Richard Twiss, Lakota Sioux
and theologian of "First Nations,"
preferring this term to "Native American,"
writes in *Christ and Whose Culture?**
"Maybe God did bring white people over,
but it was supposed to be something mutual."

Brian McLaren, Christian author activist,
now sees the Bible as writings
from a tribal people
who suffered oppression by
aggressive neighbors and found
in God "one who loves each small tribe
as much as each powerful nation.

I look out the porch window as I read.
One great lilac bush fading,
one small sparrow pecking,
a swarm of dragonflies searching,
and a beautiful yellow tiger butterfly
fluttering.

This is our world.
Now we know
all are dependent on each other.
Let it not be too late.

* Sojourners June 2009, p. 24+

APOLOGY

I must decline the "forward" offer.
Even in the dead of winter,
I cannot imagine getting 36
more books, even free.

I know, I could give them away,
but then there are the six friends
I would have to puzzle
from my email list for days
to decide who would want them,
having to select six more,
ad infinitum.

Next there is the problem
of copying the letter.
My penmanship is terrible.
I used to print them, but no longer.
My fax copier is unreadable and
I don't know how to replace ink.

Shall I go on, dear friend?
I can bless this heat and the fan
above my head,
that this is the best place to be
even though I dread
disappointing thee.

I'm not sure that our prayers
will find a cure for cancer,
but the burning candle is beautiful
and the sentiments expressed,
though weightless,
carry much freight.

Shall I send you another poem,
a real one that still doesn't rhyme?
I'll send it in the mail
to make up for all your time.

I wrote it in Angola waiting
for my cousins before breakfast.
There were only four of us,
not at our harmonious best,
I have spared you the friction
with only a hint of the rest:

WILL I REMEMBER?
August 2009

Will I remember the last reunion
in Angola, New York?
You can sure bet on that!
Our numbers had dwindled to four
and we switched special events
from Alice's place in Green Ridge to Elmira,
and for one day instead of two.

Wilma scraped off the skin
from her upper left limb
while reaching for the cat
and falling over a table of glass.

Dee came to my rescue
as I stumbled and flew through the air.
Hearing sudden steps behind her
she caught me in time, but my shoulder still hurts.

We barely missed a storm
inspecting Erie Canal locks
and hunted forever for a
noted luncheon spot.

Not enough time to explore Elmira
to everyone's satisfaction,
but the ride both ways is still
an attraction.

Wilma's garden I have already explored,
yet a poignancy remains.
Will we see it again?
Where will Wilma be living next year?
Indeed, where will each of us be
and will our numbers drop to three?

Whatever the numbers or place,
we have had many a joyous embrace.

TO MY HOSTS: ANGELA AND JESSE

Did I forget to say "Thank you"
as we said our goodbyes?
Shame on me for missing
blessing such fine fare
I'm unlikely to get elsewhere.
What a delightful treat
for Mother's Day
this grandmother had.
I was invited for a meal,
not expecting a gourmet treat,
mango topped swordfish
in place of meat!
Thank you!

Such skills and artistry
you have to delight the eye
as well as gratify cravings
for food and good company.

JESSE'S TANK

Three fish of varying size
whose breed I do not know
swim in a pristine tank.
This pool of fish
adds more beauty
to decor of fine taste
in the rest of house.

But what intrigues me more
is the elegant bridge
for Pisces to explore
made of shiny pitch black grains
chiseled from granite pieces
used just as broken
from a construction ditch,
an ancient token
of creation's store.

BILLOWING CLOUD

There is a simple painting
hanging in front of my bed.
I bought it at a charity auction
years ago.
A great white cloud
expanding above desert land
touched with spring green
seemed to say late in my journey here,
"Life is not over."
And so I was born again in '93
when I was 69.

Retired as librarian in the East, I wandered
until volunteering in Phoenix for refugees
of war torn Central America.
The artist hung around our office,
a young man torn between
his paint box and pen.
Opting for journalism,
he left for Northwest,
and I lost track of him.

I wanted the billowy cloud on
cover of my second autobiography
telling of rebirths
to symbolize my storied lives.
But where was the artist-writer
to apprise and permission obtain
to acknowledge this worthy gift?

When I checked the Internet
his name was listed not
in Phoenix or as writer,
but full time artist in Albuquerque
depicting glorious landscapes
of a West I had left behind.

He too had found his muse
and been born again.
Tom Blazier, I acclaim you
still in your prime
this spring of 2009.

OH, ISABEL!

I knew you such a short time,
a few years, maybe three?
We met at church,
our senior Keenagers possibly.
Monthly meetings October to
June; speakers on travels,
hobbies and history
keeping us alert and in touch.

Then the monthly book group called by you,
taking us to ancient China
in *Snow Flower and the Secret Fan*;
Three Cups of Tea for today's Afghanistan,
Great Depression circus life in *Water for Elephants*,
and *Life of Lucy Larcom*,
local nineteenth century feminist.

Closer contact was choir,
I, new alto, grateful for
you at my side,
always in tune; rhythm in tact.
Best of all was Trinity's
"Journey of the Spirit"
with Tuesday winter meetings
at the pastor's house.

We could share more than most
while I drove you to and from.
What a brave spirit you were
with cane to ease your steps
more slowly in later months.

As illness took over,
you came when you could, but
increasingly stayed home,
and then the hospital times.

But I will see you often
in the empty chair where
you used to sit at Coffee Hour
ready to greet any in line
with a friendly smile and
merry glint in your eyes.

Thank you, dear Isabel,
for ringing a new "Bel" in our lives.

PERFECT PERCH

I sit quietly by my Sometime Stream.
White blossoms on tall stems
watch me from the compost pile.
I wait.
I listen to water tumbling
steadily through rocks,
birds of all sorts calling across the bursting trees.
A pair of cat birds pick across the ground
as white throats search without a sound.
When I turn my head, a red squirrel
peaks over hummock and scampers off.

.

I remember another May morning
wandering down a broad stream
lined with trees and birds,
a meadow beyond.
With camping friends and Donald,
I gloried in the peace of watching
our migrating feathered friends.
I could have watched forever, but
others were eager to move on.

Now I'm here in the woods
behind my house on a perfect perch
to watch, listen and oh, whiff the scent
of tiny blossoms and damp earth
to which I can return
again and again.

Book Three
Silver Linings

THE SILVER LINING

I was over eighty
when I made the last trip
to Mexico with the dream
of two whole weeks in Oventíc
watching a mountain community
of rebel Zapatistas
conduct a school for teachers,
run cooperatives for weavers
and video production.

But in ancient San Cristóbal
I tripped on a curbstone
and injured my knee
sending me back to Arizona
without reaching my goal.

Deciding I was no longer
spry enough for such adventures
I returned to Gloucester, Mass.
to be near my family
permanently.

The specter of old age hung,
something to shun,
but a long icy winter
captured my pen,
dismissing the dark cloud
with a silver lining
and I was alive
again.

THIS IS THE SPOT

Ambling through Ravenswood
this mild autumn day,
one of few this year
after the long severe winter
and a watery summer,
I stopped along the path
below the Hermit's plaque
listening to gurgling water
I have often passed.

"This is the spot," I thought.
It brings me back
to numerous wooded hikes
both alone and with others
here and abroad.
What a treasury of memories!

The course feeds through
a culvert under the road
and winds down a narrow channel
hampered by sturdy rocks
and stretches of grass
then disappears around a bend
hidden by low growth still green.

Above are spindly columns
of bare trunks reaching skyward
where lingering rust and gold
defy approaching cold.

I no longer dread winter's spread
despite its confining nature.
Last year's bounty
revealed new life for me.
I wait to see
what more is in store.

DEAR, DEAR FRIEND

Oh, my friend, you are so troubled.
So much pain to endure
So many cords to untangle
So many decisions to make.

Life doesn't get easier,
does it?
The years gone by
should have helped
to prepare you.
Something must have
slipped through the cracks?
Yet, we must struggle on.

From where will help come?
The mountain trails you used
to hike with loved ones
are far away.
But remember them
and some joy will creep through
to brighten a gloomy day.

You may be lonely
though others are all around.
Let not your heart be troubled.
Write it down.

Those you would like to see
may have other cares to attend.
Still, they think of you
and pray you feel God's grace
hovering wherever you are placed.

As for me,
I can give you nothing better
than the joy we have shared together
knowing whose presence
is with us always
no matter what our trials.
Hold tightly to that,
dear pretty, kind, bright
and loving friend.

God's peace be with you,
Margery

MY LOCUST TREE

Through the dining room
and porch windows
my locust tree is
turning golden now.
Wispy fronds droop
almost to the ground.

From earliest days
I worried in case disease
would conquer it,
but like me, this lacy shade
has survived each scourge.

Barring some catastrophe
it will last the winter
and bloom again next spring
soaking up whatever sunlight
seeps through the crowded maples.

Hail to you
flourishing friend!

SOMETHING NEW

I discovered
I like the view
from my front upstairs
bedroom window.

For many years
I had slept
in a ground floor room
unlike upper flats
of my childhood.

Now the scene from high
above the street
gives perspective not visible
from lower ground.

* * *

Then there is my new cubby.
It's tucked in a corner
of the living room.
now empty of heavy furniture,
but carpeted in new tufted
blue and cream.
It's bounded by tall white bookcase
rescued from the street
and a table of local history books
with lamp and writing space between.

If I run out of ideas that inspire,
looking up are scenes from the past
urging me on—
mostly filled with trees and snow.
But Wilma's Phoenix garden scene

frames one end
while Jean Collet's invitation
to afternoon tea at Ritz Collet
anchors the other.

ASK MR. WALTON

I tread carefully
so no rock or root will trip me
on the leaf covered path
although the rusty way
is brightened by dim western sun
reflecting off fallen foliage.

The silence
except for remaining leaves
rustling in the wind
and an occasional bird call
summons my attention.

I stop often
attracted by newly vacated spaces.
Changing views entrance me,
feed my hunger.
What have others felt
in this no longer
primeval place?

What was it like
when these rocks were formed in heat,
followed by frigid eons
and later melting snows
bringing gigantic boulders,
great monuments to the past,
to rest upon this ground?

What can you tell me, Mr. Walton
as I stand at the crossroads
near your cabin's plot,
your home in the wilderness
for thirty-three years?

Skip what you observed
living here alone so long.

I have read the charming tales
of your animal friends,
changing seasons and
botanical discoveries.
But tell me
what you thought
of how all this came to be
and of eternity.

ORION'S RETURN

I saw Orion tonight
rising over the cemetery hill.
Eleven-thirty was too late
to ask my new friend
to join me.

How long must I wait
to celebrate winter's new show
across the harbor horizon?

It will be a night to remember
sharing our elation
over God's creation.

CROWS CALL

The call of crows
this chilly autumn morning
reminded me of
vees of geese
that used to signal
time to load my car
and wander afar
for winter in the West.

Through rolling fields
and purple peaks
I drove until out
of desert sands
Phoenix arose,
a hive of activity
spurring my life anew.

But it was not geese
making a long flight,
just common crows
that stay around
to clean the streets.

Now I too remain nearby
stitching pieces together.
Will they make a seamless whole?
Old grief, foreign adventures,
and angels when I need them
make a lively story, but
I do not yearn for glory.

Knowing I have touched other lives
as they have touched mine
in a quest for the best
we each can do
is more than enough.

It would be great to know
the good bestowed,
but the doing satisfies.

MOONLIGHT SONATA

Remaining leaves
rustle against moonlit clouds
thin enough to reveal
glistening granite boulders
holding up the little brown house
perched above,
cuddled by woodland.

I stand on the back step
with brisk air
kissing my cheeks
remembering a hayride followed by
cider, donuts and storytelling
in an old barn crouched beneath
a harvest moon of sixty years ago.

My new friend
thought I was too aloof
for a hayride partner.
A year passed before
he returned my invitation,
but patience pays.

It was another year
before we wed,
built our own little house
on flat ground
once a peach orchard.

We planted two locusts,
three fruit trees,
a walnut and sturdy oak,
three birches, a sweet gum
and yews all around
as well as two sons
and a daughter.

Beethoven plays on
as Orion, then Sirius appears.
What a night.
What a life!

NOVEMBER 2009

I could never say
how much along the way
was meant to be
a sign for me.

Sunlit trees reflect
in mirrors of swamp water.
Rocks and dead leaves
mark the line
between yours and ours.
What does that mean
between you and me
who both inherit the sky?

The train chugs
long past these borders
and cars murmur distantly too,
but no noise is made
by the slowly sinking sun.
Maybe we just don't have
ears to hear and
must decide in silence.

RUBIES IN HIDING

I thought of you this morning,
dear ailing friend,
as I walked through the fields
on the way to the beach.
I gazed at the distant shoreline,
framed by clear water and blue sky,
then glanced down to keep from stumbling.
Tiny rubies strung together
by a slim branch
caught my eye.

Brilliant red in the sunshine,
they had remained sheltered
beneath green leaves
of the now bare bush
only to sparkle
when their cover
had been ripped away.

Through storm and snow assaulting,
they remain until time
makes them ripe to fall.
Let their beauty sparkle.

SILVER SHEATH

A silver sheath
full of love
from above
crosses the sea
beneath a somber sky.
It will carry me
through the day
along a troublesome way.

What comfort
What assurance
What strength it provides!

A gentle wind
breathes in my ear
past my cheek and
pushes me on to more
than I can perceive.

EARLY BLESSED ASSURANCE

Blessed assurance has come to me
since I was eleven.
It began on Adams Street
beneath a horse chestnut tree.

In anger, anguish and inner turmoil
I struggled over family troubles
dreading to cross the street
and climb the stairs
to our apartment.

Then suddenly I felt a presence
walking beside me.
"Let me help carry your burden,"
it said and then promised,

"Be patient; your trials
will prepare you for a mission
when you are grown."
My spirits lifted
and I walked across the street.

I COULD WRITE A HUNDRED POEMS

First frost greets the day
clear and blue
across the bay
with specks of snow
on leaves beneath my feet.

My spirits rose with thoughts
of last night's meeting.
Advent is here!

YOU MUST WAIT

You must wait
You must wait
You must watch and listen.
It will not be too late
to open the door.

Today, tomorrow
in joy or sorrow:
give and receive
a smile,
a word,
a face to remember
in this place
where you are.

It may not be
what you expect,
but wait and surrender
your will, your dreams
to what is intended.

God's love is eternal.

RAVENSWOOD HAVEN

Eager to be in the woods
I find each step up the hill
along the street tedious
until I stop to look or take a breath
and see craggy boulders
climb the hillside outlined by fallen leaves
and hazy sky.

How long was the slow motion of building
these remnants of a glacier long ago?
What a grand sight and roaring sound
it must have made
if we had the patience with earthbound eyes
to invade their action.

Now we wiggle and squirm
to endure each tiny change
or struggle in vain
to halt the future.

To be here today (tomorrow there may be snow)
is God's harvest gift for the winter inside.
I cherish these moments wondering what is ahead,
what is new, but so old
when all is said.

The moss and lichen spread upon ancient rocks,
how long before they took hold?
I hope that nothing but wind and rain
disturb this terrain.

And what is this blossom doing here?
A tiny white cinquefoil
in a cluster of dry red leaves
among rambling twigs needle thin.

If I look hard
miniscule red buds along the stems
prepare for next year.

Now that I am far around the bend
from brief encounter,
I must stop to take stock
of those moments while pondering to myself,
no, I must not go up the trail
that leads along the fortress wall.
It is too rugged for now faltering footsteps
though a shiny stream beckons.

I repeated my thoughts aloud
to a lone hiker strolling toward me.
Reticent as usual, her solo reply,
"Oh? – Enjoy your walk,"
and on she went.

I felt slighted, but
perhaps she too was
lost in contemplation,
my interruption no elation.
I must not complain
as I have had the silence I sought.
Even the usual dog walkers
have left me in peace.

Those varied green splotches
on rugged terrain
through barren trees is moss
on rock-formed moraine
a verdant reminder
of spring to come.

As I scribble such trivia
a massive eratic [2] appears
among the rubble
with a reminder that no matter
how weak my efforts, they
are part of a whole
and may be improved upon
by others – or myself.

---

2   a rock pushed out of place by glacier

RED VELVET

I was looking for a pin one day,
too much trouble to go upstairs
where I kept them in a dainty
china covered container.
Maybe there were some
in the sewing box downstairs.
Yes, I spotted the round, red velvet
pin cushion with its secret bottom
compartment.

Memories flooded from the treasure
I used to hide inside –
nickels and dimes I earned running errands
for neighbors when we were poor.

My cache of small change
transported me on Saturday afternoons
from sordid childhood
to the magic world of movies.
Adventurous cowboy serials in the West
or curly Shirley Temple childhood troubles
cheerfully solved, delighting everyone
through the Great Depression.

Our shabby two-room apartment
was furnished with one three-drawer dresser.
The top one was mine,
filled mostly with underwear.
The innocent pin cushion was hidden below
among other keepsakes.

Slowly the errand money accumulated
until I counted four dollars and thirty-three cents,
some of them were coins found in the street.

One day I eagerly pulled off the red velvet top
ready to remove one dime
for the Saturday matinée
only to find it was almost empty!

I was heartbroken.
Who but my dad in his need for a drink
could have stolen my hard earned savings?

There are many things I regret
about our relationship,
that red velvet pincushion being but one.
It reminds me that never once
did he return anger
for the resentment I harbored.
Dad may have spurned being Christian,
but his actions were more Christlike
than mine.

MOONLIGHT WITH WILMA

When I awakened last night
a silver sphere shown through
the spruce peaks and across the lawn
over a thin layer of snow.
My back windows brought the haunting light
onto the cedar chest below
across the floor
and all the way to the door
begging my attention.

No howling wind broke the stillness,
but thoughts of Wilma, alone as I,
maybe awake, grieving more loss,
wondering what the future could bring.

What can I offer? Maybe a poem?
Two lines from one, "You must wait –
Your must wait" are not much of a
start, but you must wade
through the sorrow for more.

My hope chest is full of yesterday's dreams,
but also warm blankets when needed.

AFTER THE STORM

Is the storm over?
The half moon in dark sky
shines brightly through a halo
of fluffy clouds hurrying by.

Before me, melting snow gurgles
as it rushes down the street,
and empties through the grate
at my driveway's edge.

I step carefully over the slippery walk
before the snow bank halts me.
How fresh and invigorating the air.
I am alive once again.

The gloom has lifted
after today's start on bio for publication
and copying poems
of my return home from hospital
for Bonnie just back from surgery.

Yes! This contents me now—
taking small steps
to share God's love
eternal for all.

SPRING SUNSET FOR PRISCILLA
April 23, 2010

The sun is setting through the trees
directly over the hill behind our backyard.
It is gone before I can sit to eat,
but a pale yellow glow still reflects
off a cluster of small clouds.
Stately, graceful tulips by the rock wall
have closed for the night
while daffodils and forsythia linger
either side of fresh green lawn.

Early spring has crowned our day,
a foretaste of new life for Priscilla Homans Lane.
We celebrated this gentle soul
in words and music
of family, pastor and friends followed by
conversation and a tasty collation.
.

As a mother, grandmother, companion,
community and church participant,
her earnest character and tranquil beauty
were illumined through different points of view.

Priscilla, we will remember you more clearly
seeing you as others have
in different settings, earlier times.
May your spirit continue to refresh
and shine wherever it flowers.
Thank you for your presence among us.

HALF MOON BEACH

I have not walked this stretch of beach
in many months.
I have not swum in these chilly waters
for several years.
Still the beauty of the place
captures my soul in its embrace.

When Gloucester was my fair weather home,
not long after dawn
I'd check the tide upon the rock
where I would shed my shoes and socks
to be sure I could dry my feet
after a bracing swim.

I would dip my toes in the salty sea and then decide
whether they would warm or freeze.
Once satisfied,
slowly lowering my body into the stream
I'd swim from side to side
keeping my eyes upon the shore
for twenty minutes or more.

I gloried in the freshness of the morning,
my private paradise
bounded by granite crescent arms,
lofty oaks upon the bank
and maybe a cormorant off shore.

They say you should not swim alone
but I never felt in this Godly place
my life was threatened
and I would rather drown in the tidal sea
than be stricken in basement
where none could see.

So I have survived those years
of glorious swims
that cooled me for sweltering days.
I live here now all year long
and can be entranced above the beach
coated in winter garb with icy strands
dripping off the rocks,
snow laden sand and leafless oaks
looking out to sea.

DEATH OF A TREE
February 26, 2010

Our big spruce was blown over
in a storm last night.
When I went to bed,
lightening bolted over
the hill across the street.
The trees and ocean
were howling like never before.

I wondered if I would be able to sleep.
Even the windows creaked.
Should I move to the front bedroom
where there were only two
instead of five? I decided not.

As the clamor increased
I crawled out from the blankets
made my way in the dark
to back windows and saw
the two commemorative spruce
frantically waving
in a cloudlit sky.

The house shook,
but I heard no resounding crunch
over the noise of wind and waves.
Maybe vegetation where
the larger tree landed
cushioned the sound
for when I sat up in the morning
an ominous void had replaced
the giant plant's station
of eighty years.

And then I discovered a huge boulder
just below the overturned root.
It was almost as large
as the only other gift
of the glacier in our yard.
The spruce had left its own tombstone!
Compensation for damaging the granite wall
which sheltered buried tulip bulbs?

I grieve for the fallen tree,
the crumbled wall
and the vulnerable bulbs.
I wonder what will fill this space?
But life has a way of mending
that I am willing to embrace.

EMPTY SPACES

What can I say
about this day
that gives so much satisfaction?

The tree is gone
but time will speed
before rock garden replaces
shattered wall.

Nevertheless the void creates
a view of spring green foliage
brightened by setting sun –
a more spacious yard - yet cozier,
embraced by surrounding growth.

Like our lives when we let go
of long cherished habits, possessions, –
fresh opportunities are invited,
a broader outlook with new connections.

The rhythm of my life has altered.
God's gifts are seen more plainly.
The days rush by but the unexpected
rewards more than day I planned.

OPPORTUNITY

Leave loathsome tasks alone
when here at last
opportunity shines.

Why scrape the bottom of the bowl
while along the rim
the best to taste
with lips alone.

Poets delight in pithy print
slough off the lint.

POSTSCRIPT:
I MUST WALK IN THE RAIN

I must walk in the fresh spring rain.
What a blessing it brings
both to earth and soul.

The shower had passed
by the time I left home,
the pavement was still wet.
Drops remained on bushes
as I trudged up the hill.

I walked this road
one day last week.
As I stopped to absorb
the gorgeous spring offering
full of lush new growth,
a rare car approached
with window rolled down.
The face looked familiar,
but I wasn't sure until
a young woman called out,
"Margery?"

What a delightful surprise!
It was Amy who used to live
on a meadow around the bend.
I couldn't believe that ten years had passed
since she moved away.

A sister lover of the earth,
my neighbor had returned
and was creating another
environmentally friendly habitat
across the Cape near Halibut Point.
I must visit her, she urged.

In sunshine or rain I never know
what surprises may come
when I walk this heavenly road.
Returning down the hill, I stopped.
There was my silver lining
stretching across Eastern Point
past the ocean below layers
of quietly moving clouds.

Later it occurred to me,
every dawn brings a silver lining
to whatever darkness
we carried into the night
and is more precious
than the most golden sunrise.

Readers Comment

Dudley, Celeste–"I can't tell you what a comfort and pleasure it was to have your books come today . . .[they] brought tears to my eyes."

Grannis, Margaret–"Long Icy Winter poems . . . are an exquisite integration of physical (visual), mental, emotional and spiritual beauty. You have captured the essence of human warmth and divine wisdom . . .I found myself weeping tears of joy, sadness, and recognition as I read them."

Haverly, Ferd–"Your heart and soul shines through your poems."

Kelly, Judge James–"It is your eloquent telling that opens to others nature's joys."

McKay, Priscilla–"After reading your 'Half Moon Beach' poem so many times I want to tell you how much I really enjoy it. . . ."

Robinson, Myrtle–"Thanks for words of hope. I have read both several times."

Ronan, John–"Margery Leach's poems are heartfelt and sincere. She brings a bright, mature hopefulness to . . . nature and life."

Simon, Art–(Founder of Bread for the World)–"My wife and I read them with much pleasure and appreciation the way in which you express yourself, so simply and with beauty of words."

Van Gunten, Sarah–"I loved this poem ('Death of a Tree') . . . very visual imagery, and I felt every shake of your house."

Valley Religious Task Force Central America Night Tribute to
Margery
[volunteer of the year]
February 27, 1998

Margery

Dust devil in Dodge Colt packed with cross country gear whirling into CAMBIO office, full of faith, power and no-nonsense New England purposefulness. Doing what has to be done. No hesitancy. Straight ahead. Doing God's work with an energy and enthusiasm that inspires and awes. Sleeping on the muddy, cold ground of the Chiapas highlands, waltzing with Leroy in front of the federal building, sticking, licking, stapling, risking, loving, telling heartfelt stories of the man she loved but never letting the past hold her back or the danger beyond the next turn of the jungle path intimidate her.   Quick to laughter. Ready to encourage. Defiantly standing up to the darkness with a faith and strength that will not be denied.

Thank-you Margery,
Adelante!
Ferd Haverly
Former Director of CAMBIO/
VRTFCA

www.ingramcontent.com/pod-product-compliance
Lightning Source LLC
LaVergne TN
LVHW091259080426
835510LV00007B/330